A souvenir guide

Prejudice & Pride

Alison Oram & Matt Cook
Foreword by Sarah Waters

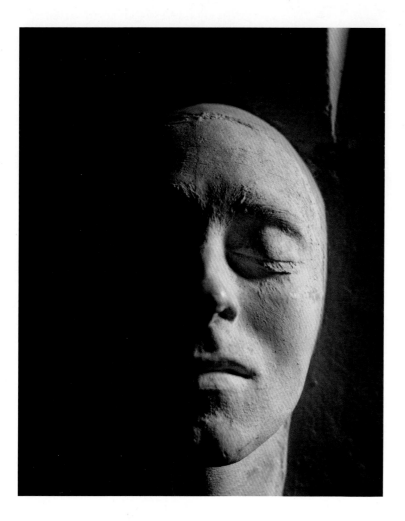

National Trust

A Fuller Picture

by Sarah Waters

Back in 1989, a fresh-faced 22-year-old, I visited Sissinghurst Castle Garden with my first girlfriend. We went there not for the glorious garden itself, nor for the wonderful setting, but because we knew that its one-time owner, Vita Sackville-West, had had many affairs with women. As we wandered about, I remember that we weren't quite daring enough to hold hands. But I still recall the thrill we felt at discovering this semi-secret bit of 'our' history.

Left *Orlando on her return to England*. Vita Sackville-West posed for this illustration for Virginia Woolf's novel: 'I was miserable, draped in an inadequate bit of pink satin with all my clothes slipping off, but V[irginia] was delighted and kept diving under the black cloth of the camera to peep at the effect' (NT 3220860)

These days we can all be a bit bolder about exploring and enjoying the UK's rich heritage of sex and gender diversity. And I'd argue that without an awareness of that heritage our experience of certain National Trust properties is incomplete. It can only add a fascinating layer to our sense of the history of Ickworth, for example, to know that John, Lord Hervey was often absent from the family home, pursuing passionate male friendships elsewhere. It surely enhances our visit to Knole to picture Vita Sackville-West 'stalking' down the gallery 'in her Turkish dress' as she flirtily showed off the house to Virginia Woolf. And to tour Woolf's own country home, Monk's House, without acknowledging the fact that so many of its illustrious visitors over the years were, like Woolf herself, bisexual or gay – people like Lytton Strachey, Duncan Grant and E.M. Forster – is to fail to appreciate the full boldness of the artistic and political unorthodoxies for which the house served as a haven.

An attention to LGBTQ (Lesbian, Gay, Bisexual, Transgender, Queer) history can also make us sensitive to the fashions, styles and traditions that have gone into the shaping of Trust properties. A homosexual scandal in 1841 forced William Bankes to flee the country, but his continuing devoted curation of Kingston Lacy and its collections reminds us of the influence that homoeroticism has had on ideas about art history. In a similar way, the paintings and stage designs of Oliver Messel on display at Nymans testify to the important longstanding connection between gay men, costume and

Above The Elizabethan tower at Sissinghurst

performance. At Plas Newydd, Henry Paget's lavish affection for glorious high campery bankrupted the estate, but his conversion of the family chapel into the Gaiety Theatre hints at how adept LGBTQ people have been at putting their own particular stamp on the properties they've inherited, overturning conventional expectations with distinctly queer agendas.

And what of the LGBTQ experiences of the other, less visible residents of Trust places, the servants, the gardeners, the chauffeurs? Most of their stories, alas, like other working people's, have gone unrecorded. But to acknowledge the queer potential of the past is to open a space for their recovery. It's to find figures with the power to shock, surprise, inspire and move us. It's to build a fuller, more fascinating picture of how the nation's historic properties have been used and shaped by their owners and occupants and left for us to enjoy.

Tackling Prejudice and Celebrating with Pride

by Rachael Lennon

In December 2016, the National Trust launched *Prejudice & Pride*, a year-long exploration of LGBTQ heritage across England, Wales and Northern Ireland.

Fifty years after the partial decriminalisation of homosexual acts, celebrations and commemorations are taking place to mark the lives of people who challenged conventional notions of gender and sexuality. LGBTQ heritage is an important part of all our history and, like today, many National Trust places were the homes and workplaces of members of an LGBTQ community.

Events will be taking place across National Trust properties, from Kingston Lacy in Dorset to Hadrian's Wall in Northumberland. For the first time, the Trust will have a widespread, national presence at Pride festivals. We are publishing new guidebooks and online resources and releasing a podcast series to shine a spotlight on these histories. Some of our stories are relatively well known; others have remained hidden until now.

Prejudice & Pride will help to demonstrate how deeply and widely LGBTQ heritage goes back into our shared history. We are working with a number of communities, artists and creative practitioners to breathe life into our places, collections and stories.

Prejudice & Pride is also part of a broader programme that explores the different and less told relationships between people and places.

The legacy of the programme will grow in years to come as we continue to research and better understand these histories; as we invite in Stonewall and other partners to reflect on our work, and as we partner with Historic England to relist buildings in our care to reflect more strongly their LGBTQ heritage. We are committed to ensuring that the National Trust protects and shares these wonderful places for ever and for everyone.

Below **Kingston Lacy**

Thinking Queerly

Left William John Bankes, who transformed Kingston Lacy from his forced exile in Italy; painted about 1833–6 by George Hayter (Kingston Lacy; NT 1257128)

What are we looking for in tracing queer histories through the properties and collections of the National Trust?

Firstly, we are looking for people connected with those properties and collections who were intimate – emotionally, sexually – with people of the same gender. This did not make them gay as we have understood that identity for the past 50 years. It did not even make them homosexual – an identity term inaugurated in 1867, but not popularised until much later. These individuals may not have attached a label or even a sense of sexual identity to their desires and intimacies, however central they were to their lives.

Though men have always had intimate relationships with other men, and women with women, these have been understood differently at different moments and in different places, and have only recently been seen as one side of a gay/straight binary of sexuality. This makes us cautious in approaching the queer past – we are not looking for gays and lesbians in history, but for signs of same-sex relationships and desires and their different configurations. We use 'queer' in this guidebook to describe this sense of divergence because it means eccentric, odd or askance as well as designating homosexual love and desire. We do not use it to mean a specific identity like gay or homosexual or trans, but rather to suggest same-sex intimacies and gender crossings which can't be tied down or understood through this more contemporary language.

This brings us to the second thing we are looking for: that is places, architecture, design, and objects which people may have associated with themselves as a way of articulating (tacitly or explicitly) and legitimising their desires and relationships. Classical and Hellenistic sculpture recalled a time when relationships between men were judged differently. Gothic art and architecture might refer to hidden secrets and delights. Modernism suggested a new openness and a rejection of outmoded conventions and moralities. Queer desires might in these ways find a heritage, a culture and an identity through such traditions and objects – and the stories told about them.

The people we discuss in this guidebook are mainly those who had the money and status to live, build, design and collect in these ways. As we wrote about them, we were aware of other queer lives lived around them which left little or no trace. Their shadowy presence suggests that the queer histories and associations of the National Trust are even richer than we have been able to present here.

People and Places
Men, Women, and Herveys
John, Lord Hervey

JOHN, LORD HERVEY *Lord Privy Seal* in the Reign of KING GEORGE II

In 1735 the poet Alexander Pope published his *Epistle to Arbuthnot,* an infamous attack on John, Lord Hervey (1696–1743) of Ickworth, Suffolk.

Hervey featured in the poem as 'Sporus', a boy whom the Roman emperor Nero had castrated and then taken as his wife. Pope castigated Hervey for his sexual ambivalence:

Fop at the toilet, flatterer at the board, [who] now trips a lady, and now struts
    a lord

Left John, Lord Hervey holding his purse of office as Lord Privy Seal; painted by J.B. Van Loo in 1741 (Ickworth; NT 851778)

Right John, Lord Hervey; bust by Edmé Bouchardon, 1729 (Ickworth; NT 852228)

Above *The castrato*; detail from scene 4 in William Hogarth's *Marriage à la Mode* (Hanbury Hall; NT 413864)

Right Mary Lepel, who married Lord Hervey in 1720 and bore him eight children; painted by Johann Zoffany (Ickworth; NT 851998)

In the 1730s Italian castrati such as Carlo Farinelli were the sensation of the London musical scene. Farinelli was praised for the purity of his singing voice, but was attacked as unmanly and unBritish by William Hogarth in his cycle *Marriage à la Mode*.

Pope's vicious satire on Hervey shows how effeminacy could be used to deride queer men in terms of their indeterminate gender. An accomplished politician, Hervey wore white make-up, was a fop, endured chronic ill-health and was subject to fainting spells – all fuel for attacks on him. Even his close friend Lady Mary Wortley Montagu observed of him: 'The world consists of men, women, and Herveys', thereby suggesting that queer men were a kind of third sex. Indeed, attempts were made to discredit Montagu herself as a lesbian or sapphist, probably because she was an adventurous traveller and independent thinker in an age when gender roles were being challenged and realigned.

'A bug with gilded wings.'

Alexander Pope on John, Lord Hervey

Categorising John Hervey is complicated. Today we might call him bisexual. In 1720 Hervey married Mary Lepel, with whom he had eight children. She was left alone at Ickworth (or in their London town house) for long periods after Hervey met Stephen Fox,

a country squire and later peer, in 1727, with whom he had a fifteen-year relationship. Hervey commissioned Hogarth to paint a portrait that celebrated this intimate friendship. The painting, which hangs at Ickworth, is now difficult to interpret, but the ties of friendship it records may also have been masonic.

Cross-dressing
Chevalier d'Eon

A celebrity in his own lifetime, the gender-nonconforming Chevalier d'Eon (1728–1810) was a French spy, diplomat and soldier. The Chevalier lived the early part of his life as a man, and in later years as a woman.

D'Eon served as an officer in the Seven Years War, and was sent to London as a diplomat in 1763, where he was involved in complex political intrigue. From 1770 there were rumours that d'Eon was a woman and constant speculation and wagering about d'Eon's sex. Huge bets were placed, crowds would gather if d'Eon was recognised, and she no longer felt safe on London streets.

There is no record of d'Eon having any sexual or romantic involvement with either men or women. In 1771 Washington Shirley, 5th Earl Ferrers, invited d'Eon for a long stay at Staunton Harold, his country estate in Leicestershire. Such allies could prove important in queer people's lives. Between 1771 and 1777, d'Eon spent nearly half his time on the Ferrers estate. D'Eon became a close friend of Shirley, who had also been in the military, and these long retreats to the country made life bearable.

In the late 1770s, d'Eon returned to France to live as a woman, but came back to London in 1785 and lodged with an admiral's widow. She earned money by various means, including fencing tournaments. On d'Eon's death in 1810 her body was found to be that of a biological male.

Various traces of d'Eon's life can be found in National Trust collections. D'Eon archived his life and wrote obsessively. Such self-description of their presence in the world has been important for many queer people. Early copies of d'Eon's memoirs are held in the libraries of five National Trust properties, showing that d'Eon was a celebrity whose story excited the public. The most tantalising fragment is a 1778 pamphlet held at Dunham Massey, which appears to refer to d'Eon's gender transition.

Above The Chevalier d'Eon fencing (British Museum)

Opposite The Chevalier d'Eon in 1792; by Thomas Stewart (National Portrait Gallery)

Gender-crossing was also found among ordinary folk. Jockey John (or Jockey Jack) worked as a jockey racing at Nottingham courses and served as a groom in the 1770s–1782 at Calke Abbey, Derbyshire. On his death in a Nottingham workhouse in December 1797 it was reported that:

A pauper died in St Mary's Workhouse who had resided in it a considerable time and had always been regarded as a male and the father of a family of several illegitimate children, having been sworn to him, who on being laid out was found to be unmistakably a woman. She had formally figured on the turf under the cognomen of 'Jocky John' and had been a Groom in the service of Sir Harry Harpur.

It was not uncommon for gender-crossing or 'masquerading' to be reported in ballads or the press, and women who had passed as men were often regarded with respect as well as astonishment.

We do not know how Jockey John felt about his gender and gender crossing. It may have related to a need or desire to work and earn in particular ways; to a wish to be part of that family; or to a feeling that he was a man. The paucity of sources – especially about working-class lives – makes such questions of motivation and feeling very hard to answer.

A Louche Disposition
Thomas Patch

The elite male tradition of the Grand Tour of Europe was well established by the early eighteenth century. Such tours exposed rich and aristocratic young men to classical and Renaissance art and culture in Italy, and encouraged a British passion for these periods and places.

Others had less high-minded interests. The aesthete Horace Walpole derided the Dilettanti Society as 'a club, for which the nominal qualification is having been in Italy, the real one, being drunk: the two chiefs are Lord Middlesex [of Knole] and Sir Francis Dashwood [of West Wycombe Park], who were seldom sober the whole time they were in Italy.'

For some, these tours also provided an initiation into homosocial and perhaps homosexual hedonism, which the painter Thomas Patch satirised in works such as *A Punch Party* (1760), on display at Dunham Massey in Cheshire. Patch has been described as 'an intelligent and original artist with a sharp eye and a louche disposition'. In 1755 he was banished from Rome by the Inquisition supposedly for having sex with other men. Patch was depicted by Johan Zoffany ostensibly admiring a painting by Titian in the Uffizi Gallery in Florence, whilst slyly pointing towards a statue of two muscular and nude wrestlers. In his *Advice on Travel* of c.1766, the Scottish painter, connoisseur and tour guide William Patoun warned visitors to Florence, 'A Certain Mr Patch at Florence is a ____'.

Thomas Patch, *A Punch Party* (Dunham Massey; NT 932354). Patch included a caricature of himself in the bust on the right-hand wall

A Careful Antiquary
John Chute

John Chute (1701–76) was the youngest of ten children, and so can have had little expectation of inheriting the family country house, The Vyne in Hampshire. Instead, he set off on a comprehensive Grand Tour of Italy in the early 1740s. Here he encountered Horace Walpole and the poet Thomas Gray, who became close friends. In most respects, they were very different. Chute was cautious and timid and a martyr to gout, which he treated – unsuccessfully – with a diet of milk and turnips. But like Walpole, Chute never married, instead surrounding himself with a circle of younger men. His effeminate streak was exaggerated by his fan and eye-glass.

Chute was a member of Walpole's Committee of Taste, which advised on the design and decoration of Strawberry Hill, Walpole's villa in Twickenham, south-west London. Strawberry was a pioneering essay in the Gothic Revival style, echoes of which can be seen in the Strawberry Parlour and the Chapel at The Vyne, which Chute finally inherited in 1754. But it would be wrong to assume that Chute was devoted exclusively to the Gothic style in the changes he made to the house. Rather, he adopted a Romantic antiquarian approach, carefully researching the past history of the house before acting.

Left John Chute; by Johann Heinrich Muntz, 1756 (The Vyne; NT 719371)

So, for instance, he considered Gothic and even chinoiserie schemes for the Staircase Hall before settling on the present classical design, which pays tribute to John Webb's seventeenth-century work on the house. The Tomb Chamber commemorates Chute's most famous seventeenth-century ancestor, Speaker Chute.

Above The Staircase Hall at The Vyne

Left *Trompe-l'oeil* vaulting painted by Spiridione Roma in the Chapel at The Vyne

Better be Dead
Edward Onslow

The fashionable new public spaces of Georgian towns and cities – assembly rooms and theatres, public gardens and picture galleries – encouraged sociability. But sociability could excite passion, and if this passion was for the same sex, then disaster could follow, as the sad case of Edward Onslow demonstrates.

The Hon. Edward (commonly known as 'Ned') Onslow (1758–1829) was the second son of the 1st Earl of Onslow of Clandon Park in Surrey. According to the historian of the family, C.E. Vulliamy, early portraits show Ned as having 'a rosy, smooth, well-rounded and amiably stupid

face; not in the least remarkable'. He had a wide circle of friends: James Stephen (Virginia Woolf's great-grandfather) judged him 'a man generally esteemed and regarded, both in public and private life; the more so because his manners and conduct formed a contrast with those of his father and elder brother, who were deservedly disliked and despised.' Ned seemed destined to go into the family business of politics, when in November 1780 at the age of 22 he was returned as MP for Aldborough. But within six months, a moment of madness obliged him suddenly to give up his seat and to flee the country.

On 3 May 1781 the *Morning Herald* reported the course of events:

An affair of the most indecent nature occurred yesterday at the Royal Academy Exhibition; a certain young man, the son of a Peer, was detected in the attempt of an infamous familiarity with a Gentleman [an Irishman named Felix McCarthy], whose indignation was so roused that the honourable aggressor was obliged to run out of the house with the execrations of the whole company.

The newspapers covered the story at length, but without being explicit about what exactly had happened. To make matters worse, the assault had taken place in public with several witnesses, in broad daylight, and in the presence of ladies: Onslow had been talking to the Keppel sisters, famous society beauties, only moments before the attack. The previous year, the Royal Academy had moved into grand new galleries in Somerset House and was keen to establish its summer exhibitions there as respectable parts of the London season.

Above *Connoisseurs examining a collection of George Morlands;* by James Gillray, who frequently caricatured gallery-goers (Osterley Park; NT 771647)

Left Edward Onslow; pastel painted by Anna Rajecka, Mme Gault de Saint-Germain about 1800, when she was also living in Clermont-Ferrand (NT 1441474). This portrait was rescued from the Clandon fire in April 2015

Nevertheless, when Onslow entered the House of Commons the following day, he received a supportive response from his fellow MPs. The Prime Minister, Lord North, also stood by him. However, by the following week, public opinion, fed by the newspapers, had turned decisively against him. Anthony Storer wrote to Lord Carlisle:

As for poor Onslow, it is all over with him, and he had better be dead...

He has made his confession to his father, and is gone off. He acknowledged that the passion he felt was beyond all control, and considering the place, the person, and all the circumstances it must have been no less than frenzy by which he was actuated, otherwise it would have been impossible to have believed either the charge or his confession.

Right Edward Onslow is probably the seated figure on the left, painted in pastel by Daniel Gardner about the time of the Royal Academy scandal (NT 1441467)

Despite the shame that Ned had brought on the family, he remained on good terms with his father, who bought him an estate near Clermont-Ferrand in France – a precondition of his marriage in 1783 to Marie-Rosalie de Bourdeilles de Brantôme. There he remained for the next five decades, surviving the French Revolution, living the quiet life of a French country gentleman, and fathering four sons and a daughter. His eldest son, George, was a distinguished composer, whose nine symphonies earned him the nickname 'the French Beethoven'.

A Gothic Recluse
William Beckford

William Beckford (1760–1844) was painted in 1781–2, around the time he came of age – the very picture of the debonair and arrogant young gentleman (now at Upton House, Warwickshire). He could afford to swagger as the heir to a vast sugar fortune founded on slave plantations in the West Indies. It was also at about this time that he embarked on a liaison with the young and beautiful William ('Kitty') Courtenay. When the affair became public knowledge, Courtenay's uncle, Lord Loughborough, launched a press campaign, which hinted at homosexual acts. Beckford avoided prosecution, but was ostracised by polite society and was obliged to flee abroad.

While in exile, he published his atmospheric and influential Gothic novel, *Vathek: An Arabian Tale*. Beckford felt safe enough to return to England in 1796, but for the rest of his life lived as a recluse. However, this did not prevent him ploughing his huge fortune into creating Fonthill Abbey in Wiltshire. With its 82-metre-high spire and vaulted octagon, Fonthill combined Gothic fantasy with awkward reality: thanks to the architect's use of shoddy materials, the spire collapsed not once, but twice.

Left The debonair young
William Beckford; by George
Romney (Upton; NT 446699)

Right One of the 'Altieri' Claude landscapes from William Beckford's collection; now at Anglesey Abbey. (NT 515656)

Below The *pietra dura* table top from Fonthill Abbey; now at Charlecote Park (NT 532954)

The baronial hall, which would have honoured the signatories of the Magna Carta (from all of whom he claimed descent), was never built. More successful was the 3.6-metre-high wall he erected around the estate to keep out the curious. He employed young male servants, but had to be careful to avoid those who had got wind of the Courtenay scandal and sought to blackmail him.

Despite the scarcity of guests, Beckford filled Fonthill with fabulous and diverse collections for his own enjoyment: famous Old Master paintings such as the Altieri Claudes (now at Anglesey Abbey in Cambridgeshire), lavish lacquer and ormolu-mounted ceramics, bronzes and heraldic stained glass. His books included the library of the historian Edward Gibbon. Inevitably perhaps, his extravagance eventually outran his income, and he was forced to sell the abbey and most of its contents in his lifetime. The building – never very real in the first place – has now vanished, and its furnishings were scattered in a series of auctions. Among the bidders were George Hammond and Mary Elizabeth Lucy of Charlecote Park in Warwickshire, who came away with a massive *pietra dura* table top, which now dominates the Great Hall at Charlecote.

Father of all Mischief
William John Bankes

William John Bankes (1786–1855) belonged to the generation that was inspired by Fonthill Abbey, William Beckford's Gothic fantasy in Wiltshire (see p.16). Indeed, as a young man, he had visited Fonthill in secret. While a student at Trinity College, Cambridge, Bankes became a close friend of Lord Byron, who christened him the 'father of all mischief'. Bankes had a reputation for extravagance and the income to indulge it.

During the Peninsular War he travelled through Portugal and Spain, buying Old Master paintings of the highest quality, which were to adorn what became the golden Spanish Room at his family home, Kingston Lacy in Dorset. He also made two pioneering expeditions up the Nile, reaching as far as the Second Cataract and bringing back an obelisk and a mass of other ancient Egyptian antiquities, together with scholarly notes on what he had seen.

In 1833 Bankes was arrested for an indiscretion with a soldier in a urinal outside parliament. He was acquitted, thanks in part to the support of the Duke of Wellington and many other influential friends, but the scandal left him little option but to retire from public life. (He had succeeded his father as Tory MP for the county seat of Dorset in 1832.) Bankes retreated to Kingston Lacy, which he inherited in 1834 and where he consolidated his vast collections of art and artefacts. With the help of the architect Charles Barry, he set about transforming the house from a red-brick Restoration mansion into a Chilmark-stone-clad Venetian Renaissance *palazzo*. In September 1841 he was arrested again for 'indecently exposing himself with a soldier of the Foot Guards in Green Park'. He fled the country, making over his estates to his brother George, but continued – at a distance – to add to his collections at Kingston Lacy. He also devised new decorative schemes, including lavishly tooled leather wall-hangings from the Palazzo Contarini in Venice for the Spanish Room. He had to enjoy his creation vicariously, but may have made a final secret visit to the house in 1854, shortly before his death.

Right William John Bankes;
by George Sanders, 1812
(Kingston Lacy; NT 1251251)

Opposite The lavishly
gilded ceiling of the Spanish
Room at Kingston Lacy

Left Simeon Solomon, *Night* (Wightwick Manor; NT 1287901)

Indecency in a Public Place
Simeon Solomon

A fate similar to William Beckford's befell the Victorian painter Simeon Solomon (1840–1905), but with much more desperate consequences. Solomon's Jewish heritage informed his early work, which included _The Mother of Moses_ (shown in 1860 at the Royal Academy, where it was praised by Thackeray: 'A more touching, a more impressive domestic group it would be impossible to imagine').

Under the influence of the Pre-Raphaelite painter Dante Gabriel Rossetti, he began treating themes of sexual desire with a poetic sensuousness that has little equal in Victorian art. Typical is _Night_, a watercolour that probably dates from the early 1870s (Wightwick Manor, West Midlands). In 1873 he was arrested for indecency in a public place and sentenced to 18 months imprisonment. This was later reduced to a term of police supervision on payment of a surety of £100. The following year, he was arrested in Paris and again given a prison sentence, and fined. Barred from the Royal Academy and all the other respectable exhibiting societies, and shunned by most of his former artist friends, he gradually slipped into destitution. In 1880 Rossetti was appalled to discover that Solomon had been admitted to hospital 'not only ragged but

actually without shoes'. In the 1880s he was reduced to living in a central London workhouse, but despite growing alcoholism, he continued to paint similar subjects, which were much admired by Oscar Wilde and his circle. At the time of his death in 1905, Christie's sold one of his paintings for £250 – an indication of a renewed and growing interest in his work.

Below Simeon Solomon, c.1866; photographed by Frederick Hollyer

Romantic Friendships
Jane Carlyle and Geraldine Jewsbury

Jane Carlyle (née Baillie Welsh) (1801–66) moved to Cheyne Row in Chelsea, west London, in 1834 with her husband Thomas (1795–1881), the essayist, historian and biographer. Carlyle's House became well known as a literary salon – with many writers and thinkers gathering there or passing through.

Amongst them was the novelist Geraldine Jewsbury (1812–80). She and Jane struck up what has since been described (not least by Virginia Woolf) as a passionate romantic friendship which lasted until Jane's death in 1866.

Letters between the pair signal the depth of their affection – and also the points of tension. Geraldine cut a more radical eccentric literary figure in London – often wearing men's clothes, smoking and espousing the controversial view that men and women should be equal in marriage, something she did not observe in the Carlyles' union. Jane meanwhile took a relatively conventional role in her marriage, which was affectionate but also fraught with argument and jealousy (on both her and Thomas's parts). Geraldine's affairs with men and women – sometimes platonic, sometimes not – also infuriated Jane.

Jane and Geraldine's relationship may not have been sexual and indeed such romantic friendships were sometimes a loosely acceptable way for middle-class and elite women to express their love for each other – especially with the

Left Jane Carlyle in 1850; painted by Carl Hartman (Carlyle's House; NT 263412)

Above Geraldine Jewsbury (NT 263762)

ballast (for one of them) of a respectable marriage. (The brief romantic friendship between Octavia Hill and Sophia Jex-Blake may have been somewhat similar: see p.48.) This acceptability is perhaps indicated by the fact that Jane did not destroy or hide their correspondence, something later intimate same-sex friends and lovers certainly felt the need to do. The context of literary London was also important to this – lending a certain bohemianism and related permissiveness to friendships and friendship networks. This was an emerging part of Chelsea's reputation during the time the Carlyles were living there. Its queer dimensions became more evident amongst a later generation of artists and writers who came to live nearby, most notably Oscar Wilde.

The infrastructure and public facilities that came with Britain's growing cities brought fresh potential for cross-class and erotic meetings. Knowingly or not, Chelsea bohemians would encounter all kinds of queer people in the streets of their neighbourhood.

Below Thomas and Jane Carlyle in the Parlour at Cheyne Row in 1857; painted by Robert Tait (NT 263684)

Masquerade
The Dancing Marquess

There is a long tradition of masquerade, dressing up and costume parties in Britain's country houses – from drawing room charades to more lavish entertainments.

Queer people have often felt the need to perform – to conceal relationships and to pretend to be other than they were in order to obscure desires which were frowned upon or acts that were illegal. Dressing up – for example as iconic figures like Sappho, Queen Christina of Sweden, Salomé or the painter Van Dyck – was a way of being playful in the face of such imperatives; a way of suggesting without confessing. The professional theatre and dance worlds meanwhile offered an escape, a community of artists and bohemians, and ways of pushing boundaries or imagining difference and a different world. Oscar Wilde's trial in 1895 saw theatre and theatrical networks evoked in the courtroom and associated them directly with queer lives and emergent identities for a broader public.

Such theatricality can be found in the former residents of several National Trust properties, such as the trio of women living at Smallhythe Place (see p.34) and Henry Cecil Paget (1875–1905), 5th Marquess of Anglesey. Paget's apparently unconsummated marriage was dissolved in 1900 and we don't know if he had affairs with other men. The family papers were destroyed, but he has been described as 'a notorious homosexual' because of his theatricality, dressing-up and cross-dressing.

His extraordinary erotic snake-like dancing style earned him the nickname 'the dancing Marquess'. This obliquely associated him with the boundary-pushing styles of the Ballets Russes, which were a hit in queer theatrical networks in London, when the company visited the capital in 1911.

Above **The 5th Marquess of Anglesey dressed as a troubadour**

Opposite above **The theatre created at Plas Newydd by the 5th Marquess of Anglesey**

Paget converted the chapel at his family seat at Plas Newydd on Anglesey into a 150-seat theatre he dubbed 'The Gaiety' – a space more accommodating of Paget's flamboyance than the chapel had been (though the costumery and ritual of high Anglican and Catholic services also had an appeal for some queer people). Significantly, Paget staged plays by Oscar Wilde, again connecting Plas Newydd and his own theatre company to the queer London theatre scene. Paget toured Europe for three years with his theatre troupe – a Grand Tour in a different key and a reminder of the importance of 'abroad' for elite British people exploring a sense of their own difference from prevailing norms. Paget's flamboyant theatricality – even after the Wilde trials – suggested the sense of impunity many in the upper classes felt; it may also have been a rather brave attempt to continue to be who he wished to be in spite of dangers and detractors.

The significance of dress can be explored through the National Trust's costume collections at Killerton House in Devon, Snowshill Manor in Gloucestershire and Springhill in Co. Londonderry. They provide a glimpse of how people shaped and presented themselves through the clothes that they wore. Of course this was the case for everyone, but it was perhaps especially important for those who were trying to hide or subtly or more directly express their difference. Paget seems to have been in the latter category: he had himself photographed in elaborate historical costumes and in women's clothes.

Above Léon Bakst's costume design for Nijinsky in the Ballets Russes production of *L'Après Midi d'un Faune* (NT 3134807)

Above Self-portrait of Richard Cosway in Van Dyck dress, *c.* 1770 (Attingham Park; NT 609064)

The Triumph of Fancy
Rex Whistler

The modern murals made by the artist, illustrator and stage designer Rex Whistler (1905–44) in a number of country houses across England and Wales are a wonderful flowering of neo-Georgian style. Whistler made his name at an early age and was taken up by the aristocracy to decorate their homes, and by the associated 'Bright Young People' who partied in them. His friends in the mostly queer (a term they may have used themselves) house party set included Stephen Tennant (a fellow student from the Slade), Cecil Beaton, Noël Coward, Gerald Berners and Evelyn Waugh.

Rex Whistler was charming and attractive, and many people fell in love with him. Most of his friends and contemporaries assumed Whistler was homosexual, and he certainly had romantic involvements with both men and women. His known relationships, with women, were short-lived, but he had a long romantic friendship with Edith Olivier, a woman 30 years older than him.

Like other artists in his circle, Whistler was an enthusiast for the eighteenth century, visiting the gardens at Stowe (where his brother had been at school) as inspiration for his panoramic murals. His work expressed classical formality, but also decorative rococo flourishes.

Above Whistler posing in the manner of the eighteenth-century Rococo artist Watteau; photograph by Cecil Beaton

The execution of his masterpiece, a huge, 17-metre-long mural of an Italian seaport in the dining room at Plas Newydd, Anglesey, gave Whistler enormous pleasure. As in his other work, it demonstrates the playfulness and whimsy of Whistler's style. He incorporated self-portraits into his murals, and often the pets or children of his patrons. The jokes in his panels and allusions to contemporary life and his own affairs as well as art historical references made his work clever, delightful and amusing. His final work of this type (before he was killed in a tank battle on active service in Normandy) was at Mottisfont Abbey in Hampshire, where he painted *trompe-l'oeil* murals to evoke a medieval priory (the building's origin) with added drawing room curtains, echoing the Gothick of Horace Walpole's Strawberry Hill (see p.12).

Left Self-portrait of Rex Whistler as a gardener in the Plas Newydd mural

Above The Rex Whistler Room at Plas Newydd

Below Whistler's design for *Properties of the National Trust*

Bloomsbury Circles
Virginia Woolf

In 1919 the writers Virginia Woolf and her husband Leonard bought an unpretentious cottage, Monk's House in Rodmell, Sussex, as their country retreat from London. Virginia Woolf and her sister, the artist Vanessa Bell, were at the heart of the now almost mythical network of English modernists known as the Bloomsbury Group, a name which has also come to stand for their bohemian approach to love and sexuality. Both in their art and literary work and in their personal lives, this intricate circle of friends, family and lovers aimed to live out their principles of constant intellectual enquiry and experiment.

The domestic arrangements and interior décor (with handmade textiles and bold patterns and paint) of the Bloomsbury Group constructed a radical model of home life and desire. In their questioning of contemporary gender relations, openness to queer sexuality and grounding in the

domestic and everyday, the Bloomsbury households contributed to a very English and rather queer version of modernism.

Virginia and Leonard Woolf lived apparently conventionally at Monk's House, but at nearby Charleston Farmhouse a more radical household was forged by Vanessa Bell and her partner, fellow artist Duncan Grant, who had many relationships with other men and also fathered a child with Vanessa. Charleston operated as the country home of some other members of inner Bloomsbury, Vanessa's husband Clive Bell, the eminent economist Maynard Keynes and Vanessa's children. Their romantic entanglements and affections criss-crossed the spectrum of hetero, bi and homosexual, and in their unconventionality were deeply queer.

Vanessa Bell and Duncan Grant advised the Woolfs on the interior design of Monk's House, and it displayed their characteristic decorative panels in the dining room chairs, painted tiles around the bedroom fireplace and elsewhere, and Omega workshop-style furnishing fabrics.

Left The Sitting Room at Monk's House

Below left One of a set of six dining chairs with cane seats and backs. The oval needlework panels were designed by Vanessa Bell and Duncan Grant for the Lefevre Gallery in 1932 (Monk's House; NT 768191.1)

Opposite below This copy of the limited first edition of *Orlando* (1928) was given to Eddy Sackville-West by Virginia Woolf (NT 3220860)

Opposite Virginia Woolf; by Vanessa Bell, about 1912 (Monk's House; NT 768417)

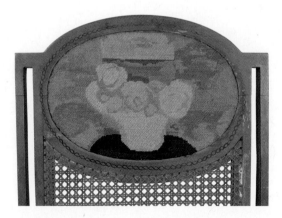

In the early 1920s Virginia Woolf met and fell in love with the poet Vita Sackville-West, and had a short but profound affair with her. This intense experience and her fascination with Vita led to Woolf's enormously successful novel *Orlando* (1928), which imagines Vita (as Orlando) living through centuries, shifting gender and commenting on the changing assumptions about love, marriage and women's role over time. Orlando's ancestral home is based on Knole, Vita's family home, and expresses her attachment to the place.

Early in the mock-biography, Elizabethan-era Orlando elopes from the frozen Thames with Sasha, a Russian princess, echoing Vita's wild abandonment of her marriage for an earlier lover, Violet Trefusis. Entering the damp and gloomy nineteenth century, Orlando is horrified by Victorian marriage and its restraints on women. *Orlando* was Woolf's most light-hearted novel, both playful and political. It mocks all the fixtures and fittings of heterosexuality – birth, marriage, and home-making, as well as conventions of sex and gender, identity and sexuality. It re-imagines the world and English history from a feminist and queer perspective.

'Whether, then, Orlando was most man or woman, it is difficult to say now and cannot be decided.'

Virginia Woolf

Creative Retreats
Judith Ackland and Mary Stella Edwards

Beyond the Bloomsbury Group, it was a frequent practice for writers and artists of sufficient means to spend at least part of the year in the countryside or at the coast, seeking creative solitude or subject matter. Some of these people fashioned beautiful country retreats where they could be themselves more freely.

One of the most special is the tiny Cabin at Bucks Mills on the north Devon coast. This was the summer home and studio of a same-sex couple – artists Judith Ackland (1898–1971) and Mary Stella Edwards (1898–1989). It has been left untouched since the 1970s. Ackland and Edwards met as art students at the Regent Street Polytechnic and lived and worked together for 60 years.

Their work is held in a number of national art collections and at the Burton Art Gallery and Museum in Bideford. Mary Stella Edwards was also a gifted poet (and was published by the Woolfs' Hogarth Press).

The Cabin occupies a prominent position above a former lime kiln and landing stage with wonderful views of this industrial heritage beach (often painted by them both).

Above right **The Artist's Cabin at Bucks Mills**

I am the lover and the loved,
The embrace I give encircles me;
And while I have scarce breathed or moved
The tide has risen over me;
I am the body of the swimmer
And the soft engulfment of the sea.

(From 'Duality', 1947)

Escaping Celebrity
T. E. Lawrence

Clouds Hill in Dorset was likewise a rough and ready bolt hole for T. E. Lawrence (1888–1935), also known as Lawrence of Arabia. Lawrence chose the place partly to escape his celebrity following his First World War achievements as a military and intelligence officer in the Middle East. The public's imagination was fuelled by media stories of his heroism and romanticised imagery of him in Arab dress.

Left below T.E. Lawrence; in 1931; photographed by Howard Coster (National Portrait Gallery)

Left The Sitting Room at Clouds Hill

Below Lawrence on his motorbike

When he found the cottage he was working in a tank corps under the pseudonym Private T.E. Shaw. Lawrence began renovating the cottage, following Arts and Crafts principles, from 1922, to be his main home. Though he enjoyed the rest and seclusion it offered, he also entertained many friends from the worlds of literature and the visual arts including Thomas Hardy, George Bernard Shaw, Augustus John, Siegfried Sassoon and E.M. Forster.

Lawrence had an enigmatic public persona. He had worked to support the political cause of Arab self-determination in the First World War and was enchanted by young Arab men. Homosexual experiences were hinted at in his writing. He dedicated his most famous work *The Seven Pillars of Wisdom* (1926) to Dahoum Ahmed, a young man with whom he had had a close and intimate friendship during his pre-war years in Syria.

An Inscrutable Mystery
Henry James

Lamb House in Rye is rather more comfortably provisioned than Clouds Hill. American novelist and critic Henry James (1843–1916) found this house in 1897 and loved it so much that he lived here for most of each year for the rest of his life.

James was a self-proclaimed bachelor, and took pains to keep his complex sexuality an inscrutable mystery, burning his letters and notebooks. He wrote effusive and erotic letters to younger men, including the sculptor Hendrik Andersen (1872–1940). The two men met in Rome in 1899 and continued an intense relationship for many years. Andersen later visited James in Rye.

'Every word of you is as soothing as a caress of your hand, and the sense of the whole as sweet to me as being able to lay my own upon you.'

Henry James to Hendrik Andersen,
August 1904

James's attempts to remain inscrutable are arguably reflected in his literary work, which often contains a gothic sense of hidden secrets. His novel *The Bostonians* (1886), for example, describes a love triangle that involved a possibly lesbian relationship between two women.

Left Henry James; by
Philip Burne-Jones
(Lamb House; NT 204159)

Rye Dissected
E.F. Benson

Among James's friends and visitors in Rye was E.F. Benson (1867–1940), author and queer son of an equally queer mother, Mary Benson, wife of the Archbishop of Canterbury.

E.F. Benson took on the lease of Lamb House soon after James's death and wrote his later novels there. He served as mayor of Rye in the 1930s, and set several of his highly popular 'Mapp and Lucia' series of novels in the town, thinly disguised as 'Tilling'. His writing pokes fun at the cultural snobbery and class-consciousness of the community.

Above Lamb House

Right E.F. Benson; by Howard Coster, 1934 (National Portrait Gallery)

Suffrage Lives
Edy Craig, Chris St John and Tony Atwood

The history of three women who lived at Smallhythe in a ménage à trois shows how queer lives are not always pursued in secrecy or isolation from the rest of society but are connected to – indeed often at the centre of – the cultural and social currents of their time.

Smallhythe Place was the home of the celebrated Victorian actor Ellen Terry (1847–1928), who bought the sixteenth-century timber-framed farmhouse in 1899 at the height of her fame. She gave the use of another house in the grounds – Priest's House – to her daughter Edith (Edy) Craig (1869–1947) and the latter's female partner Chris St John (Christabel Marshall) (1871–1960).

Edy Craig also worked in the theatre, primarily as a producer and costume designer. She was a committed suffrage feminist in the years before the First World War, when Smallhythe became a haven for many other activists. Craig founded and managed the Pioneer Players (1911–25), a theatre society that staged many innovative plays in London and produced some 150 plays for the suffrage movement. There were many lesbian relationships and networks among suffrage feminists, though, as with their Victorian 'new woman' predecessors, it is often impossible to know which specific attachments were eroticised friendships and which were sexual relationships.

Opposite The Barn Theatre at Smallhythe with Edy Craig, Charles Staite and Irene Cooper Willis; painted by Tony Atwood in 1939 (NT 1118237)

Below Ellen Terry's friendship beads, each given to her by a friend or relation (NT 1117793.1)

Right Edy Craig; painted by Tony Atwood, 1943 (NT 1118235)

Below right The Barn Theatre

Edith Craig
Aimée Lowther
Mrs. Walker
Aimée Lowther
Mrs. Watson
Aimée Lowther
Penelope Wheeler
Charles Coleman
"Tug" Fairchild
Julia Doane

Edy Craig shared a home with writer and translator Christopher St John from 1899. In 1916 the artist Tony (Clare) Atwood (1866–1962) joined the household now living both at Smallhythe and Bedford Street, London. This was on the condition that: 'If Chris does not like your being here, and feels you are interfering with our friendship, out you go!' In fact it was a very successful arrangement, as Atwood's paintings of the women at Smallhythe suggest.

Their household was constantly stimulated by literary and political visitors, many queer. Their friend Radclyffe Hall, whose lesbian novel *The Well of Loneliness* was prosecuted for obscenity in 1928, lived a few miles down the road in Rye. Also nearby at Sissinghurst was Vita Sackville-West. Chris St John, like many women, was quickly mesmerized by Vita, who granted her one night of love in 1932, which did little to assuage Chris's devotion.

Vita was of a younger generation than the Smallhythe trio and referred to them as the 'old trouts'. She was nevertheless kind to them, making sure that they were coping as they got older, and helping to transfer Smallhythe to the care of the National Trust.

One frequent visitor to Smallhythe was an old comrade from suffrage days, Vera 'Jacko' Holme (1881–1973). Jacko had worked as a chauffeur to the Pankhursts and then as an ambulance driver in Serbia during the First World War. Jacko's lesbian identity, like that of her friends, was announced through her masculine nickname, her short cropped hair and her increasingly masculine clothing.

After Ellen Terry's death in 1928, Edy Craig transformed Smallhythe Place into a memorial museum, converted an outbuilding into the Barn Theatre, and held an annual drama event from 1929. This attracted performances from many luminaries of the London theatre world in subsequent years, including their friends Sybil Thorndike and homosexual actor John Gielgud.

During the days of the suffrage struggle, Edy had co-written and produced the epic 'Pageant of Great Women' and she continued to produce pageants in the interwar years. Virginia Woolf, another Smallhythe visitor, was inspired: in her last book *Between the Acts* (1941), Woolf represents this English village tradition and may have used Edy as the model for the strange spinster Miss La Trobe, the pageant director and one of the novel's queer characters.

The loving relationship between the three women was marked as such after their deaths. Chris St John and Tony Atwood were buried side by side in the churchyard next to Smallhythe Place. Craig was not initially buried with her partners, but a matching commemorative plaque was placed next to their grave in 2012.

Dispossessed
Vita and Eddy Sackville-West

Vita Sackville-West (1892–1962) grew up in the great 'calendar' house Knole (with its 365 rooms) and wrote about it often in her poetry and prose. Her teenage romance with schoolfriend Rosamund Grosvenor was played out partly at Knole, and Vita took her subsequent lovers there to show them the great house of her ancestors, of which she was so proud. Unhappily, as a woman, Vita could never inherit Knole and felt eternally dispossessed. She belonged to Knole, but Knole could never belong to her. Vita lived with her husband Harold Nicolson first at Long Barn and then at Sissinghurst, which helped to satisfy her deep feelings of connection to the Weald of Kent.

Vita was metaphorically reinstated at Knole through Virginia Woolf's novel *Orlando,* published in 1928, the year that Vita's father died and possession of Knole transferred to his brother, who became the 4th Baron Sackville. Next in line would be Eddy Sackville-West, Vita's cousin, who ironically never liked Knole and did not have the visceral sense of belonging to the house that she did. Vita's uncle gave her a key to the garden, which was her most treasured possession.

Eddy Sackville-West (1901–65) was a homosexual, a writer and music critic. Vita's father gave him an apartment in the Outer Wicket Tower at Knole for his use when he left Oxford in 1925. Part of a kind of second-generation Bloomsbury, Eddy's social circle was full of writers, artists and musicians.

He worked to promote modern composers, including Benjamin Britten and Michael Tippett, who were both homosexual.

Eddy Sackville-West had a number of affairs with men, including Duncan Grant, the Bloomsbury sculptor Stephen Tomlin (both bisexual) and the heir to Herstmonceux Castle in Sussex, Sir Paul Latham. However, his relationships often ended in pain and unhappiness. His domestic life was more successful and he established a happy male ménage for many years from 1945. His home, Long Crichel in Dorset, was shared with the music critic Desmond Shaw-Taylor, the artist Eardley Knollys and the literary critic Raymond Mortimer. James Lees-Milne (see p.50) was a frequent visitor and good friend of many members of this circle, especially Eardley Knollys, who was the National Trust's representative for south-west England from 1942 to 1957. Eddy and his friends illustrate ways in which queer lives have often involved innovations and experiments in home and family.

Opposite Eddy Sackville-West; by Graham Sutherland, 1954 (Knole; NT 129982)

Right The Gatehouse Tower at Knole, in which Eddy Sackville-West lived

Far right The Music Room at Knole

Desiring Gardens
Vita Sackville-West and Harold Nicolson

Gardens are often associated with sexuality – as places of pleasure and repose, which reflect the cycle of nature. The Garden of Eden with its notions of innocent and sinful desire has influenced English garden design at great houses, as have changing fashions and taste in architecture and ornament.

Gardens can become material hosts for the enjoyment of queer sexualities (or indeed inadmissible heterosexual desires), hiding lovers' liaisons behind hedges and in secluded spots (sometimes designed for this purpose). They may also contain symbolic expressions of love and passion, in their planting and layout.

Sissinghurst Castle Garden has been seen as a queer garden for many years, at least by its lesbian and gay visitors. A joint project between Vita Sackville-West and her husband Harold Nicolson, and laid out immediately after their purchase of the property in 1930, the garden ostensibly symbolised their harmonious and loving marriage. It also, from the 1970s onwards, following publication of their letters and biographies, represented the now only half-concealed queerness of that marriage. Both Vita and Harold had numerous same-sex relationships during their life together; on Vita's part this included some very serious relationships – most famously, those with Violet Trefusis and Virginia Woolf.

Vita now has an established reputation as a maker of and commentator on gardens – a reputation which has lasted far longer than the recognition she received in her own lifetime as a successful popular writer and poet. The pleasure of Sissinghurst lies in its combination of distinct geometric garden

Left The White Garden at Sissinghurst

Below Vita in her garden

Opposite Harold and Vita at Sissinghurst in the 1930s

rooms with formal walkways and vistas, anchored by its central feature, the romantic Elizabethan Tower with its twin turrets, where Vita had her study. The White Garden, made in 1950, with its colours of grey, green and white, enjoys particular fame and countless replications.

Vita and Harold were strong supporters of the National Trust in the postwar years. She served on the Trust's Gardens Committee, he on the Executive Committee. But when their son Nigel tentatively asked whether she would ever contemplate giving Sissinghurst to the Trust, her response was 'Never, never, never'. However, when the garden was eventually made over, it rapidly became one of the most popular and well-visited of the Trust's properties.

Beyond the country house garden, the many open spaces in the care of the National Trust have had huge significance for queer people. For Edward Carpenter, pioneer of sexual freedom, and his partners George Hukin and George Merrill, walking around the Peak District moors was a key activity for their own queer family, their friends and their wider circle. The landscape became synonymous with notions of freedom, sexual expression and the felt naturalness of their desires. This bond with nature was also expressed in E.M. Forster's novel *Maurice*, inspired as it was by his visit to Millthorpe, Carpenter's home.

Working-class Lives

At Sissinghurst in the 1950s we catch a glimpse of relationships that were doubtless repeated on country estates all over England.

In 1957, the year the Wolfenden Report recommended the partial decriminalisation of sex between two men, two estate workers were subject to possible blackmail because of the sex they had supposedly had together. Vita Sackville-West wrote to her friend James Lees-Milne (see p.50): 'We are threatened with a police case of a criminal nature – absolutely nothing to do with me, but now it is being said "Well, if Lady N [Vita] herself ... etc. etc." I leave you to imagine the rest'.

Though it seems to have come to nothing, Vita worried about Sissinghurst 'getting a bad name' and about associated gossip surrounding her own love affairs. On this estate – as elsewhere – servants and employees held intimate knowledge of 'goings on' above and below stairs. Whilst this might lend them a certain power in a climate when queer liaisons were scandalous and illegal, their livelihoods might depend on their discretion.

Sometimes servants became trusted confidants. In other cases the employer/employee relationship might shield a love affair. At Lewes House in Sussex, for example, the classicist and collector Edward Perry Warren (1860–1928) lived for many years with his 'secretary', Harry Asa Thomas.

Non-elite queer lives emerge through stories like these and that of the cross-dressing groom Jockey John (p.9). Scandals meanwhile revealed further queer dimensions to the lives of the poor. Lambeth Workhouse was exposed in 1866 as a 'breeding ground' for 'unnatural passions'.

The Living Orlando
Gordon Langley Hall (1922–68)/
Dawn Langley Simmons (1968–2000)

Sissinghurst also marks the beginning of a life story that is all the more remarkable for breaking the conventional bounds of birth, gender, race and class. Dawn Langley Simmons (né Gordon Langley Hall) was the illegitimate offspring of Jack Copper, who worked as chauffeur at Sissinghurst from 1933.

Being brought up in a household with fluid ideas of gender and sexuality encouraged Gordon to believe that he was really a girl. 'I felt in my heart that I was the living Orlando', he wrote later.

In 1950 he moved to the United States, where (still identifying as a man) he formed a relationship with the mural painter Isobel Witney. On the latter's death in 1962 Gordon found himself a millionaire and the possessor of a 40-room mansion in the queer district of Charleston, South Carolina. In 1968 he underwent gender reassignment surgery at Johns Hopkins University hospital and took the first name Dawn. She stunned the locals yet further the following year by marrying Jean-Paul Simmons, a young black car mechanic. (The state had only legalised inter-racial marriage the previous year.)

Sadly, she endured vile racial prejudice from her neighbours and physical abuse from her husband, who was diagnosed with schizophrenia. They were divorced in 1982, but not before she had a daughter, Natasha. She also had a successful literary career as a celebrity biographer and told the story of her life in *Man into Woman: A Transsexual Autobiography.* Dawn's children's book, *The Great White Owl of Sissinghurst,* recalls her Kentish childhood. Nigel Nicolson remembered her as 'gallant, resilient and unfailingly generous'.

Left Dawn Langley Simmons, who was brought up at Sissinghurst

Right Dawn became a close friend of the actress Margaret Rutherford, whose life story she wrote

Bright Young Things
Oliver Messel

Above Oliver Messel;
photograph by Snowdon

In the 1920s the tabloid press landed on 'bright young things' as an epithet for a group of fashionable elite and artistic men and women.

Amongst them were a number of queer men – including designer Oliver Messel (1904–78), photographer Cecil Beaton (1904–80), socialite Stephen Tennant (1906–87), writer Beverley Nichols (1898–1983), and actor and writer Noël Coward (1899–1973). Well known on the London scene, they also attended lavish parties at country retreats. Tennant's Wiltshire home, Wilsford, was a frequent venue, and photographs by Beaton and others show guests in fancy dress dancing, socialising and fooling around by the pool.

Oliver Messel came from an artistic family and as children he and his siblings had been encouraged to dress up and put on theatrical productions at his family home, Nymans in West Sussex. After Messel's sister Anne inherited the house, it became a place of fantastical escape and performance (rather as Henry Paget had, a generation before at Plas Newydd – p.24).

After the devastation of the First World War this group looked to fun and the rejection of constrictive morality. The group was mixed in terms of gender and sexuality, and there was an ethos of acceptance of the desires of others.

Though the 'bright young things' may have revelled in their *avant-garde* status and perhaps also the gossip that surrounded them, country houses like Nymans were places where the conventional rules of respectability and conduct might not apply; they were not subject there to the same kind of scrutiny as on the London social scene. There are resonances here with the contemporaneous, though differently configured, Bloomsbury Group.

Oliver Messel at Nymans seems to have been relatively open with friends and family about his long-term relationship with Vagn Riis-Hansen. Avoiding scandal and skirting arrest nevertheless made discretion imperative. The pair kept separate bedrooms, for example, and even after their deaths in 1978 and 1977 (respectively) they were described as business partners and friends. Messel's siblings' more short-lived marriages were meanwhile referred to directly. The habit of discretion was powerful: queer relationships are

often understood and experienced in the context of euphemism, tacit knowledge, gossip and rumour.

In the summer of 1939 Messel masterminded the Jersey Ball at Osterley Park – a glamorous evocation of the eighteenth century and the last such occasion before the war. For Lady Jersey, who before her marriage had starred in Charlie Chaplin's movie *City Lights,* he designed a sumptuous ball gown in silver and blue silk brocade. After the war he restored another survival of Georgian sociability – the Assembly Rooms in Bath, which had been severely damaged by German bombs.

An Odd Family
Evan, 2nd Viscount Tredegar

At Newport in Wales the poet and painter Evan Morgan, 2nd Viscount Tredegar (1893–1949), was using his family seat at Tredegar House in South Wales for similarly decadent weekend house parties with numerous queer attendees.

The Morgan family was notoriously eccentric ('the oddest family I ever met', according to the Duke of Bedford), and Evan was no exception. As well as being a Roman Catholic convert and chamberlain to two popes, he was an occultist and friend of bisexual magician Aleister Crowley. Though Morgan married twice, he also had affairs with men and was principally homosexual.

His expression of his sexuality wove into the established eccentricity of his family, rather as the Messels' artistic bent gave Oliver a way of couching his queerness. Queer people might in these ways be part of family cultures rather than exiles from them.

These people were also in different ways part of the establishment – able because of their wealth and class, their country retreats, their networks, and their professional position to be queer social insiders. Messel maintained an impressive clientele for his theatre and interior design work despite the gossip that surrounded his friendship network and personal life. The same is true of designer Oliver Ford (1925–92). Ford worked on a number of country homes, including his own Bewley Court in Wiltshire and the gardens at West Green House in Hampshire. The Oliver Ford Trust has, since his death, funded a number of National Trust projects. Ford's standing was such that despite his arrest and prosecution for homosexual offences in 1969, he continued his work as interior designer to Princess Margaret and the Queen Mother. Queer people had to walk a fine line, but their queerness did not necessarily always render them outsiders.

Above Tredegar House

Opposite Viscount Tredegar in his robes as Privy Chamberlain to the Vatican; painted in 1941 by Cathleen Mann (Tredegar House; NT 1552383)

Recklessness and Ruin
Bobbie Shaw

Robert ('Bobbie') Gould Shaw III (1898–1970) was the eldest son of Nancy Astor of Cliveden in Buckinghamshire. He had survived the First World War as a hard-riding, hard-drinking subaltern in the Household Cavalry, but, like so many, was mentally scarred by the experience. He cracked his scull twice in bad falls while steeple-chasing. When drink got the better of him, he was forced to resign his commission, but the disgrace only seems to have increased his recklessness.

Bobbie was homosexual – a fact that he had kept secret from his mother and step-father. As Nancy Astor's biographer writes, 'His relations with his mother were painful and complex…. From early days he adored her, lavished on her a love that was abnormal in its extremity, and then, when he reached manhood, he came also to resent her, to react against her tyrannical possessiveness and openly accused her of wrecking his life.'

It was just a matter of time before his recklessness got him into serious trouble. In 1931 he was caught by the police committing a homosexual offence in a public toilet. The authorities gave Bobbie an opportunity to avoid prosecution, but he refused, staying to face the music, which comprised six months imprisonment.

However, as with William Beckford, power and influence could limit scandal. As the owners of *The Times* and *The Observer* (and with the support of another press magnate, Lord Beaverbrook), the Astor family were able to keep the story out of the newspapers. The house staff at Cliveden were also sworn to secrecy.

Bobbie's step-brother David Astor was the main financial backer of the Homosexual Law Reform Society from 1958 – Bobbie's experience mobilising him to a fight against what he saw as the injustice of the law. The Sexual Offences Act, which partially decriminalised sex between men in private in England and Wales, was finally passed in 1967; Bobbie committed suicide three years later. Legal redress could not ameliorate some of the crippling emotions that came with social censure.

'As a young man his wit was brilliant and devastating – sometimes perhaps too devastating.'

Michael Astor on his step-brother, Bobbie Shaw

Opposite The Astors'
palatial Buckinghamshire
house at Cliveden

Right Robert ('Bobbie')
Gould Shaw III; charcoal
drawing by John Singer
Sargent, 1923 (Fine Art
Society)

The National Trust

From its foundation in 1895, and like any major organisation, the people involved in the Trust, then as now, mirrored the sexual diversity of the wider population.

The development and concerns of the National Trust in the twentieth century reflected the interests of its founders, supporters and staff, who were anxious to preserve what they saw as Britain's finest historic landscapes and buildings for the enjoyment of the nation. Here we focus on people and groups, who, over the following century, were pivotal in advancing and changing the Trust.

Octavia Hill

Octavia Hill (1838–1912) was a pioneer social reformer and conservationist, and one of the three founders of the National Trust.

She used her skills as a manager of working-class housing to create healthier communities and trained other women to do the same. Hill was instrumental in saving open space for recreation in inner-city London; she coined the term 'the green belt' and worked with other National Trust founders to preserve the Lake District from despoliation by railway companies.

Hill's lack of interest in marriage and her passionate friendships with other women formed a life-path that was common among independent-minded Victorian women. In the early 1860s she had a friendship and shared a home with Sophia Jex-Blake, who led the fight for women's entry to the medical profession. In May 1860 Jex-Blake

confided to her diary that Hill 'sunk her head on my lap silently, raised it in tears, and then such a kiss!' Hill's biographer Gillian Darley concludes, 'While the language is that of the passionate friendship enjoyed by many innocent young Victorian women, on Sophia's part it was clearly more intense, a love affair – if only of the heart.' Subsequently, Hill's long-term companion was Harriot Yorke, with whom she lived and worked for over 30 years. From the perspective of the present day, it is difficult to interpret the meaning of these friendships, but they were undoubtedly central to Hill's emotional life.

After Octavia Hill's death, her companion Harriot Yorke and Hill's sister Emily bought Hydon's Ball and Heath in the Surrey Hills in her memory. Here, in one of Octavia Hill's most cherished places, stands a memorial stone bench. Two walking trails in the area were inaugurated as a National Trust commemoration of Hill's centenary in 2012.

Above Pastel drawing of Octavia Hill

Ferguson's Gang

The Trust was best known in its early years for its aim of preserving the countryside and open spaces of Britain, defending the landscape against industrial development and encroachment by railways, roads and urban sprawl. One of the most fascinating stories of the Trust in this period concerns the fund-raising and significant publicity achieved for its work by Ferguson's Gang, a secret society of women formed in 1928. They kept their identities hidden and appeared in public disguised in masks and costumes.

Led by 'Bill Stickers' and 'Red Biddy', the gang collected money to preserve buildings at risk of demolition, especially rural and vernacular buildings, and for the purchase of key pieces of land. Ferguson's Gang saved and restored Shalford Mill in Surrey for the Trust and held their meetings there, fortified by hampers sent down from Fortnum & Mason.

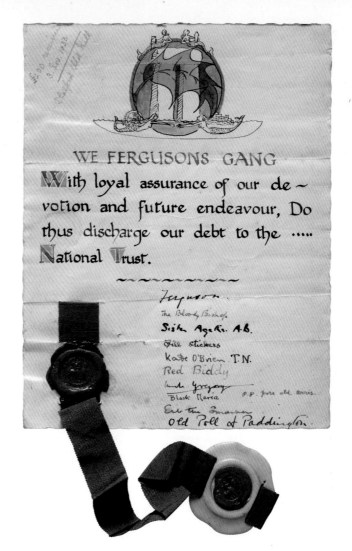

A diverse and eccentric group of independent women, several gang members had same-sex relationships as well as unconventional – queer – heterosexual marriages. Risk-taking 'Red Biddy' was the first of the gang to deliver money incognito to the Trust. Later a peace activist and GP, 'Red Biddy' (Dr Rachel Pinney) had relationships with other women from the 1940s and came out as a lesbian in later life on the 1989 TV programme 'Women Like Us'.

Above Illuminated manuscript with the seal of Ferguson's Gang

Left Ferguson's Gang calling card for 'Red Biddy' (Rachel Pinney)

Prince of Decorators

John Fowler

John Fowler (1906–77) was the most influential interior designer of his generation. He championed what came to be known as the English country house style (a subtle mixture of the traditional and the comfortable), which he applied to more than 30 National Trust houses.

He has been criticised for taking an unscientific approach to his decoration of historic interiors, and many of his schemes have since been 'defowlerised', but the best, such as Claydon in Buckinghamshire, have stood the test of time.

For his own country home, he restored the Hunting Lodge near Odiham in Hampshire, a modest mid-eighteenth-century folly in the Strawberry Hill Gothick manner, which he bequeathed to the National Trust. Of himself, he said, 'I'm an incurable Romantic, you see, although I do try to stifle it. Romantics usually get hurt'. His biographer concludes, 'perhaps had he lived in less repressive times – homosexuality was only legitimised in 1967 – his life might have been radically different.'

James Lees-Milne

From the late 1930s, the National Trust worked with the government to protect English country houses and their contents from the threat of dereliction and dispersal. An essential figure in this activity (and thus the National Trust as we know it today) was the architectural historian and conservationist James Lees-Milne (1908–97).

Lees-Milne had a profound love of the English country house and its art and architecture. He was the central force in the Trust's acquisition of some

Above James Lees-Milne in 1950

Left The North Hall of Claydon House was decorated by John Fowler in 1956–7

key country houses between the 1930s and the 1950s, charming their owners, sometimes over many years, into giving them to the National Trust.

'Jim' worked for the Trust between 1936 and 1966, advising its committees on which buildings should be acquired for the nation, and writing on the history of architecture. He was passionate about protecting what he considered the best of England's architecture. Among the houses that came to the Trust largely thanks to his efforts were Stourhead in Wiltshire, Attingham Park in Shropshire and Knole in Kent.

Lees-Milne's wonderfully acute and revelatory diaries capture the eccentricities of the country gentry and aristocracy. He moved within the cocktail party as well as the scholarly set. The diaries (now published) record his own affairs and relationships, predominantly with men, although he was also attracted to women and married later in life. Alvilde Lees-Milne, his wife for over 40 years, made gardens herself and wrote about them. She had her own lesbian backstories in both France and England.

Harold Nicolson, whom Lees-Milne first met in 1931, was one of his lovers, but also a lifelong friend and, in some respects, a mentor. Lees-Milne soon became a firm friend of Vita Sackville-West, Harold's wife, and toured potential country house acquisitions with Vita and Harold in the 1950s. Lees-Milne had been taught at Oxford by the later chair of the Wolfenden committee. He also had brief affairs with Eddy Sackville-West (see p.36) and the outwardly heterosexual Lord Arran, who was to lead the 1967 legislation to partially decriminalise male homosexuality through the Lords.

Gervase Jackson-Stops

Gervase Jackson-Stops (1947–1995) joined the Trust in 1972 and became its architectural adviser with a freely roaming role in 1975.

Jackson-Stops brought new standards of scholarship to National Trust guidebooks and published widely on architectural history. He rescued a number of significant National Trust properties including Canons Ashby in Northamptonshire and the gardens at Stowe in Buckinghamshire. The parties at his own restored historic home, the Menagerie in Northamptonshire, featured opera and dressing-up. Jackson-Stops's early death from an AIDS-related illness in 1995 was one of many such losses in the 1980s and 1990s.

Below The Chinese House at Stowe was restored in memory of Jackson-Stops

Weddings and Civil Partnerships

There are historic examples of same-sex couples improvising marriage rituals in front of small groups of friends. There are records of mock marriages taking place between men in London's Molly Houses in the eighteenth century and also among Oscar Wilde's circle at the end of the nineteenth century.

This seems sometimes to have been for fun – parodying an institution from which these couples were excluded (even if many of them had entered it with their female partners). Others perhaps saw it as a way of more earnestly marking their relationship. There were dangers attached to even such hidden ceremonies – we know about these ones only because those involved went to the pillory, gaol and even the gallows.

Recent years have seen a thawing of attitudes towards homosexuality, as shown by the British Social Attitudes Survey. Whilst 74% of people surveyed thought 'homosexual relations' were 'always' or 'mostly' wrong in 1987 (up from 62% in 1983), by 2000 the figure had dropped significantly – though 46% of the sample still agreed with this statement. From 2004 gay and lesbian couples have been able to mark and celebrate their relationships through civil partnerships and, from 2014, through marriages. By this time only around 30% of those surveyed disapproved of such relationships – though many still argued that the institution of marriage was corrupted or devalued through civil partnership and especially the further step to gay marriage.

For some couples involved, this has been an opportunity to be visible in their difference; for others it has been more about fitting in.

Several National Trust properties have hosted civil partnerships and marriages. Amongst the first to do so were Bodiam Castle in East Sussex, Osterley Park, the eighteenth-century villa in Hounslow, west London, Blickling Hall in Norfolk, Hanbury Hall in Worcestershire, and the Temple of Venus, overlooking the lake in the landscaped gardens of Stowe in Buckinghamshire.

The choice of a Trust property as a gay or lesbian wedding venue might signal a couple's stake in what the Trust represents or perhaps conjures memories of visits with family, friends and partners.

Below and left **Wedding at Quarry Bank Mill**

The National Trust Today

Artists and historians have more recently sought to explore and draw out the queerer side of the Trust's history – focusing often on the obscurity and intangibility of those threads of the past.

Art installations at Nymans and The Vyne in 2011 unravelled the houses' queer associations for contemporary audiences. The Victorian Back to Back houses in Birmingham's gay village have been a recent venue for the Shout queer arts festival. In 2016, as a marker of the queer tragedies associated with British prisons, singer Patti Smith performed Wilde's *De Profundis* at Reading Gaol. In Wilde's former cell in C block, photographer Nan Golding mounted an exhibition accompanied by the sound track of a 91-year-old man demanding a pardon for his imprisonment for homosexual offences years earlier.

In Worcestershire, Hanbury Hall has invited a number of artists to create contemporary responses to a dramatic set of murals which include depictions of Achilles and his lover Patroclus. In Hackney in east London, the Tudor Sutton House is hosting four seasons of events to showcase works by LGBTQ artists, to explore activism, to unpick fluid identities in Alice in Wonderland, and to commemorate vanishing LGBTQ spaces in London. It has also sought to amplify queer echoes from the sixteenth century though installations and soundscapes of Shakespeare's sonnets. The house's place in 1980s squatting and counter-cultural history is part of the heritage the house will showcase in 2017.

Knole, Smallhythe and many other properties are also hosting events this year as part of the Trust's commemoration of 50 years since the partial decriminalisation of homosexuality. Many gay men, lesbians and trans people work and volunteer for the Trust, and some property teams have joined local Pride events – and will again in this commemorative year.

Such events encourage us to think about the Trust's holdings and to engage in the past in different ways. If queer people have been viewed as social and cultural outliers, that does not place them outside Britain's social and cultural history, or beyond the purview of our national heritage.

They are woven into both – and have shaped material spaces, collections and landscapes, now cared for the the Trust. We understand more about how queer lives have been lived in part because of these holdings. And through an investigation of those lives, we learn more about the shifting norms and expectations queer people had to negotiate – and how they invested in and pushed against them. The properties, collections, people and spaces of the National Trust reveal some of the steps in the dance of queer and normal – a dance which was choreographed and re-choreographed across the centuries and forms part of all our histories.

Opposite In the Hanbury Hall murals, Achilles is disguised in women's dress, but reveals himself to be a man by choosing the spear and shield

Above, left to right
Oscar Wilde; photograph dated August 1892 (Smallhythe; NT 1122238)

Sutton House has a diverse programme of LGBTQ events

Rainbow nation. Colourful characters from the 2016 Birmingham Pride parade

Further Reading

Michael Astor, *Tribal feeling*, John Murray, 1963.

Polly Bagnall and Sally Beck, *Ferguson's Gang*, National Trust, 2015.

Michael Bloch, *James Lees-Milne: The life*, John Murray, 2009.

Hugh and Mirabel Cecil, *In search of Rex Whistler: His life and his work*, Frances Lincoln, 2012.

Matt Cook ed., *A gay history of Britain: Love and sex between men since the Middle Ages*, Oxford: Greenwood World Publishing, 2007.

Matt Cook, *Queer domesticities : Homosexuality and home life in twentieth century London*, Palgrave, 2013.

Gillian Darley, *Octavia Hill: A life*, Constable, 1990.

Victoria Glendinning, *Vita: The life of V. Sackville-West*, Penguin, 1983.

Rosina Harrison, *Rose: My Life in Service*, Cassell, 1975.

H. Montgomery Hyde, *The other love: An historical and contemporary survey of homosexuality in Britain*, Heinemann, 1970.

H. Montgomery Hyde, *The story of Lamb House*, National Trust, 1975.

John Ingamells, *Dictionary of British and Irish travellers in Italy*, Yale, 1997, pp.745–6 [Patch].

Rebecca Jennings, *A lesbian history of Britain*, Oxford: Greenwood, 2008.

Gary Kates, *Monsieur d'Eon is a woman: A tale of political intrigue and sexual masquerade*, Johns Hopkins University Press, 2001.

R.W. Ketton-Cremer, *Horace Walpole*, Hart-Davis, 1964.

Tim Knox, 'Gervase Jackson-Stops (1947–95)', *Architectural History*, 39, 1996.

Hermione Lee, *Virginia Woolf*, Vintage, 1997.

Joy Melville, *Ellen and Edy*, Pandora, 1987.

Thomas Messel ed., *Oliver Messel: In the theatre of design*, Rizzoli, 2011.

Lucy Moore, *Amphibious thing*, Penguin, 2000, pp.221–234 [Hervey].

Nigel Nicolson, *Portrait of a marriage*, Weidenfeld and Nicolson, 1973.

Alison Oram and A. Turnbull ed., *The lesbian history sourcebook: Love and sex between women in Britain from 1780 to 1970*, 2001.

Alison Oram, 'Sexuality in heterotopia: Time, space and love between women in the historic house,' *Women's History Review*, 21 (4), 2012, pp. 533–51.

Daniel Orrells, *Sex: Antiquity and its legacy*, I.B. Taurus, 2015.

Derek Ostergard ed., *William Beckford: An eye for the magnificent*, Yale, 2001.

Emma Slocombe, 'The reluctant heir: Edward Sackville-West at Knole', *Apollo NT annual*, 2016, pp.19–27.

Karen Stanworth, 'Picturing a personal history: The case of Edward Onslow', *Art History*, 16/3,1993, pp.408–23.

Christopher Sykes, *Nancy: The life of Lady Astor*, Collins, 1972, pp.326–7 [Bobbie Shaw].

Adrian Tinniswood, 'A Queer Streak', *The Long Weekend*, Jonathan Cape, 2016, pp.249–67.

Laurence Whistler, *The laughter and the urn: The life of Rex Whistler*, Weidenfeld and Nicolson, 1985.

Martin Wood, *John Fowler: Prince of Decorators*, Frances Lincoln, 2007.

Virginia Woolf, *Orlando*, Hogarth Press, 1928.

Left *The Terrace outside the Priest's House at Smallhythe Place*, painted by Tony Atwood, 1919 (Smallhythe Place; NT 1118216)